The Basilica
of Saint Mary of the Angels
in Portiuncula

EDIZIONI PORZIUNCOLA

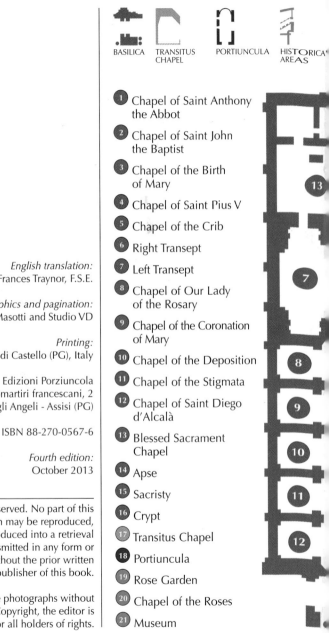

BASILICA   TRANSITUS   PORTIUNCULA   HISTORICAL
            CHAPEL   AREAS

1 Chapel of Saint Anthony
   the Abbot

2 Chapel of Saint John
   the Baptist

3 Chapel of the Birth
   of Mary

4 Chapel of Saint Pius V

5 Chapel of the Crib

6 Right Transept

7 Left Transept

8 Chapel of Our Lady
   of the Rosary

9 Chapel of the Coronation
   of Mary

10 Chapel of the Deposition

11 Chapel of the Stigmata

12 Chapel of Saint Diego
    d'Alcalà

13 Blessed Sacrament
    Chapel

14 Apse

15 Sacristy

16 Crypt

17 Transitus Chapel

18 Portiuncula

19 Rose Garden

20 Chapel of the Roses

21 Museum

English translation:
Sister Mary Frances Traynor, F.S.E.

Graphics and pagination:
Lelli&Masotti and Studio VD

Printing:
Studio VD – Città di Castello (PG), Italy

© Edizioni Porziuncola
Via Protomartiri francescani, 2
06088 S. Maria degli Angeli - Assisi (PG)

ISBN 88-270-0567-6

Fourth edition:
October 2013

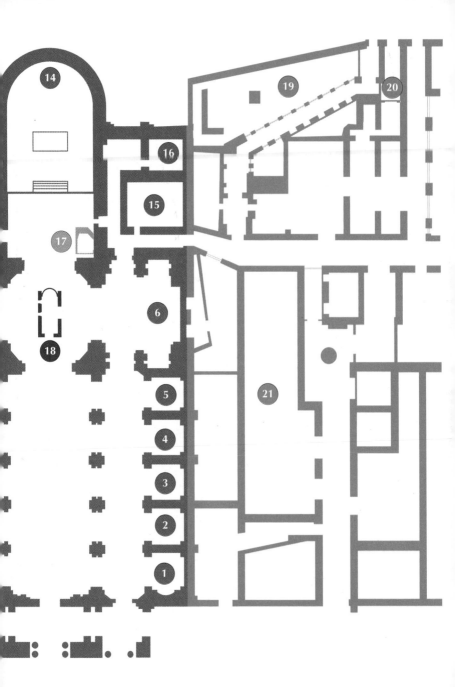

Introduction

In the plain below Assisi, between 1569 and 1679, the Patriarchal Basilica of Saint Mary of the Angels in Portiuncula rose up solemnly and majestically, to enclose the places marking the life and death of Saint Francis.

At the center of the great temple is the little Benedictine church from the ninth century, called Portiuncula. When Francis arrived here at the beginning of the twelve hundreds, the humble and secluded church dedicated to the Assumption of the Blessed Virgin Mary was surrounded by an oak woods and was in a state of almost total abandonment. Francis repaired it with his own hands and it became the point of reference throughout his life and that of his brotherhood. It was here that 25-year-old Francis, listening to the Gospel, finally understood his vocation. He renounced the world to live in radical poverty and began to dedicate himself to an itinerant apostolate. At the Portiuncula, the Saint received the first brothers and founded the Order of Friars Minor and in 1211, with the clothing of Saint Clare, founded the Order of Poor Clares.

Here the Saint celebrated the first "Chapters" (general meetings of the brothers) and from the Portiuncula sent his followers as missionaries of peace to people of the whole earth. At the Portiuncula, Christ appeared to Francis granting, through the intercession of Mary, the extraordinary indulgence of the "Pardon of Assisi" (1216).

Within the apse of the Basilica is the Transitus Chapel , where Saint Francis – on the eve of October 3 1226 – "embraced death singing".

To the right of the Basilica are the Rose Garden, where the tempted Saint threw himself among the thorns, and the Chapel of the Roses, the place in which Francis allowed himself a brief rest during the night.

Of particular spiritual, historical and artistic importance are the Museum and the magnificent Basilica enriched with numerous masterpieces, including frescos, paintings, statues and precious works in wood.

Sac: Ædicula   Portiunculæ

et Conuentus à Ser:co Præ constructus

The primitive convent of the brothers around the Portiuncula (Reconstruction by FRANCESCO PROVIDONI, 17th century)

Where everything began

The Basilica of Saint Mary of the Angels – built starting in 1569 – rises as a great jewel-case that encloses two of the most precious treasures of Franciscan origin: the little church of the Portiuncula, the center of the entire life of Francis and of his brotherhood and the Transitus Chapel, where Francis passed from this world to God the Father.
In 1216 Pope Honorius III (1216-1227) granted Francis the plenary indulgence for all who would visit the Portiuncula on August 2nd. The "Feast of the Pardon", as it is commonly called, spread the fame

and holiness of Francis and drew ever-growing numbers of pilgrims from all parts.
The term "Portiuncula" literally means little part, little portion of earth.
In his biography dedicated to the Saint of Assisi, Thomas of Celano wrote that Francis came to a place called "Portiuncula", where there was an ancient church dedicated to the Mother of God, that was in ruins, and that the same Francis restored it with his own hands. It became the first headquarters of the Friars Minor. Pressed by the need to find a little church and a poor dwelling for his companions, whose number was increasing day by day, the Saint turned to the monks of the Benedictine Abbey of Mount Subasio. In 1209, they gave the Chapel and the wooded area surrounding it to Francis, to use. It was exactly here that Francis settled with his first followers: Bernard of Quintavalle, Peter of Catanio, Giles, Rufino, Leo, Masseo, Sabatino, Morico, John of the Cappella, Philip Longo, Angelo of Tancredi and Silvester.

A little church became the center of Francis' life and that of his brotherhood. The saint and his first companions left from here to go on long journeys of evangelization. And they always returned here.

At the beginning of the XII century, the little church of the Portiuncula had fallen into ruin and it was Francis who wanted to rebuild it. In this place, the longing for paradise was reawakened in the Saint of Assisi. Everyone knew this. Simone Weil, a Jewish philosopher who was fascinated by Christ, wrote in his autobiography: "While I was alone in the little chapel of Saint Mary of the Angels, something stronger than me, caused me to kneel down for the first time in my life".

The Portiuncula Chapel (from the X-XI century), although having been altered in various ways throughout the centuries, today still maintains its original appearance. The small size has remained untouched: about nine meters long and four meters wide. Some things have been changed (the three windows were chronologically different and the pointed barrel vaulted ceiling, which is rather accentuated in height, was most probably not the original); but, just the same, the little place holds the same fascination as it did eight centuries ago.

The Portiuncula, therefore, is a privileged place of Franciscan memories, because it preserves the life and history of the Saint of Assisi, rendering the message of faith alive and real.

D. BRUSCHI,
*The "transitus" of
Saint Francis,* fresco
on the outside
wall (1886).

The Transitus Chapel, instead, takes its name from
the place in which St. Francis passed from his
earthly life into eternal life. It was exactly here
that he wanted to be placed to die "naked on the
bare earth". The Chapel was built to preserve the
memory of the Poverello. It was the infirmary in
which the Saint died. There have been numerous
modifications throughout the centuries, which have
mostly destroyed the original walls that embraced
Francis while he was dying. The friars, however,
wanted to preserve one wall that is considered the
most precious remembrance of the "Transitus". That
wall, even though it has been tampered with many
times and even covered over and hidden from sight,
has always been cared for throughout the centuries,
because it "marks the exact place of the Transitus"
(A.M. Romanini, cit., p.85).

*Thomas of Celano
wrote: "Francis came
to the locality called
the Portiuncula, where
there was an ancient
church in honor of
the Blessed Virgin
Mother of God, that
was abandoned and
neglected. Seeing it
in such a ruined state,
he was moved with
compassion because he
had a great devotion
to the Mother of all
good. The Saint took
up his abode here and
finished repairing the
church in the third year
of his conversion.*

The Basilica

At the request of Pope Saint Pius V (1566-1572), in 1569 the construction of a great Basilica, projected by Galeazzo Alessi (1512-1572), started on the place in which the Portiuncula Chapel and the Transitus Chapel stood, as well as other remnants of the life of Saint Francis. The work was destined to contain and protect all Franciscan remnants and to receive the numerous pilgrims who came from all parts to visit them. Notwithstanding the hostility of many of the brothers, who saw the poverty desired by Francis threatened by the building of the great Temple, the decision to start the construction was based on a practical reason. Frequently, the great number of pilgrims had to attend celebrations outside the Portiuncula exposed to the sun and rain, and they often sought shelter in the Convent. The need to have a suitable space to receive them, therefore, became a necessity. The work began on the 25th of March 1569, the Feast of the Annunciation. Given the poverty of the Order of Minors, the cost of construction was assumed by the Holy See; the offerings of the

The magnificent dome rises on an octagonal drum. It is seventy-five meters high, up to the cross. It was designed by Galeazzo Alessi and was finished in 1679.

faithful and the Municipality of Assisi were also added to this donation.

At the death of Pius V, Pope Gregory XIII (1572-1585) was favorable to the building of Saint Mary of the Angels.

The work on the Basilica proceeded very slowly, for various reasons. First of all, there was the need to progressively demolish the ancient buildings and then replace them with the new structure. There was great doubt and extensive debate about the shape of the apse, so much so, that the work was interrupted from 1615 to 1622; the dome was only completed after the middle of the century. The plan of Alessi, characterized by rigorous simplicity, was an architectural expression of the Franciscan ideal of poverty.

The church, with three naves, has a transept and a dome placed at the crossing, that rests on a tall octagonal drum opened by windows on every side; the apse is semicircular.

The cornerstone of the Patriarchal Basilica of Saint Mary of the Angels was laid by the Bishop of Assisi, Mons. Filippo Geri, on March 25, 1569: this church, which protects the much smaller one of the Saint, makes it much easier to manage the flow of pilgrims which crowd into the Portiuncula each year, especially in August, drawn by the promise of the plenary indulgence, the famous, "Pardon of Assisi".

There are five chapels along each of the lateral naves which are reached through other large arches.
The strong earthquakes that hit Umbria between the end of 1831 and the beginning of 1832 caused severe damage to the Basilica, so much so that it was feared that the dome

The building of the Basilica continued until 1679 and of the two projected bell towers, only the right one was built. In 1832 an earthquake caused the façade to collapse as well as the central nave, but miraculously the dome remained intact, continuing to protect the Portiuncula.

Above: Large cloister of the Portiuncula Convent and the seventeenth century well, attributed to G. Alessi.

would collapse and ruin the Portiuncula. Pope Gregory XVI gave a notable personal contribution to the reconstruction project. Reconstruction continued for several years, rendering the entire building stable and seismically safe. The Basilica was reopened for the worship of the faithful on September 8, 1840.

The huge Basilica of Saint Mary of the Angels, which contains the Portiuncula, is 115 meter long and has three naves.

THE FAÇADE

The façade was reconstructed according to the plan of Cesare Bazzani (1873-1939). As a great supporter of the monumental style, the project was carried out with a certain ornamental richness.

The first stone was laid on April 19, 1925, despite great perplexity on the part of the public who considered the architectural grandeur totally incompatible with the ideals of moderation so typical of Franciscan buildings. Besides the numerous sculptures, the façade was enriched with an imposing gilded bronze statue of the Blessed Virgin Mary, by the sculptor Guglielmo Colasanti.

The new façade with its colossal dimensions (about 52 meters high and about 60 meters wide) was inaugurated on June 8, 1930, declaring the architectural undertaking of its author. Finally, in 1960, Engineer Giuseppe Nicolosi completed the flooring made of an enormous 700 square meter rectangle of red porphyry and travertine.

Below: a view of Saint Mary of the Angels in a photo from the beginning of the twentieth century. Today, as in the past, the "beautiful dome" of Alessi , towering above the vast plain, continues to remind us that it was here that Francis, in penance and prayer, heard from the Our Lady of the Angels that the Portiuncula would become the "door to eternal life".

The façade of the Basilica was modeled upon the Roman baroque style with a portico and balcony for blessings.

Statues of Saint Francis and Saint Clare.

The Portiuncula

he interior of the Basilica, 115 meters long, is divided into three wide naves; there are five chapels in each of the lateral ones, which over the course of more than a century were painted by numerous artists from Umbria as well as from outside of Umbria.

At the center of the cross rises the majestic dome planned by Alessi, which seems to symbolically enclose the most precious architectural relics of Franciscan origin, the Portiuncula and the Transitus Chapel. The little church of the Portiuncula has a hut-like façade on whose peak stands a gothic-style structure of unknown era in which there is a copy of a statue portraying "Our Lady of the Milk" (the original is in the Museum). It is from the Sienese school from the thirteen hundreds. On the façade there is a fresco portraying Saint Francis imploring Jesus and Mary to grant the Pardon. It was done in 1829 by Friedrich Overbeck. This painting replaced the frescos done in 1639 by the Assisi painter Giorlamo Martelli. Above the door there is an inscription in Latin that says: "This is the door of eternal life", while another inscription on the threshold says: "This is a holy place". Both of them recall how Francis felt and how he considered this church to be a piece of heaven on earth and therefore worthy of all love, honor and

The church of the Portiuncula The façade is dominated by the fresco painted by Friedrich Overbeck in 1829, depicting Saint Francis imploring Jesus and Mary for the Indulgence.

The gothic-style niche placed on top of the little church at some unknown time contains a copy of the statue of "Our Lady of the Milk". The original is kept in the Portiuncula Museum.

veneration.

On the right side there are traces of two frescos of the Sienese school from the fourteen hundreds; they depict Saint Bernardino and the Blessed Mother with Child enthroned between saints Francis and Bernardino.

Also, on the right wall there is an inscription from the thirteenth century marking the death date of Blessed Peter of Catanio, Francis' second companion (after Bernard of Quintavalle) who, upon returning from the Holy Land, died on March 10, 1221 and was buried in the Portiuncula.

On the back side there is a fresco depicting the Crucifixion. After the restoration work of 1998, this work was attributed with certainty to Pietro Vannucci (better known as "Perugino"), who worked between the XV and XVI centuries and is

considered the greatest Umbrian painter.
This work was known to exist due to a citation
made by Vasari, who recalled that the master
worked in the area of Perugia: "... particularly
in Ascesi at St. Mary of the Angels, where he
frescoed a crucified Christ with many figures on
a wall behind the Chapel of the Blessed Mother
which faces the brothers' choir".
During the same restorative work, the roof of the
Chapel was cleaned which brought to light red
and white stones arranged in geometrical designs,
with eight-pointed stars and checkered squares.
The Chapel is entered through thirteenth century
weather-beaten doors; the interior has the form of
a high pointed barrel vault.
The Portiuncula seems to transmit the incessant
echo of the prayers of the Saint and of the first
generation of Franciscans who lived here and

*Francis gathered
his brothers at the
Portiuncula to continue
their formation, discuss
the new way of life
that would become
the definitive Rule of
the Order and hold
General Chapters.
The most memorable
General Chapter
was that of 1221
when more than five
thousand brothers
participated; all of
them were lodged in
straw huts that were
provided for through
the generosity of
the local people.*

LThe painting by Ilario da Viterbo, painted in 1393, is located above the altar of the Portiuncula. The various scenes recount the vision that Francis had and the granting of the Indulgence by Pope Honorius III. The painting was recently restored and the splendid original colours have been recovered.

were happy to possess God alone.

The warm walls that transmit peace and mercy have been made smooth and polished by devout hands that for centuries have come to draw from God's inexhaustible fountain of Pardon and grace. But, the masterpiece that illuminates the poor church with bright colors is, without doubt, the magnificent painting depicting the Annunciation and the

Francis throws himself into the thorns to get rid of a temptation.

Mary is seated on her royal throne and is holding the Book of Scriptures in her left hand, while the Angel Gabriel announces to her that she has been called by God to become the Mother of his Son.

Story of the Pardon of Assisi, by Ilario da Viterbo (1393).

At the center of the painting is the scene of the Annunciation. Just as the yes of Mary at Nazareth determined the fulfillment of our salvation, the yes of Francis and Clare at the Portiuncula, the new Nazareth, caused a new season of salvation and grace to reflower for all of humanity.

The scenes that surround the Annunciation tell the story of the Pardon of Assisi. On the lower right, Francis is throwing himself naked among the thorns to overcome a violent temptation. Immediately

above, Francis, with roses in his hand, is accompanied by two angels toward the Portiuncula. Above is the magnificent scene of the apparition of Christ and the Blessed Mother to the Saint who is kneeling before the altar of the Portiuncula, offering a crown of roses to Christ and Mary.

On the left, going down, the Poverello is imploring the Holy Father Honorius III to grant the Indulgence.

At the bottom, the Saint is on a pulpit at the side of the little church, along with the Bishops of Umbria, announcing the extraordinary privilege

The Saint, on the pulpit with the seven Umbrian Bishops, is holding a white paper in his hand, which says: haec est porta vitae aeternae. He is announcing to the people gathered at the Portiuncula that he has received the grace of a new Indulgence from the Lord Jesus. The little chapel of the Portiuncula is painted on the right.

Here the Blessed Virgin, with a mantle completely damasked in gold, is seated on her royal throne. Mary's soft, serene face expresses all of her beatitudes as she invites all to adore her Son.

of the Pardon with the famous words "My Brothers, I want to send all of you to Paradise!" For a long time, the altar piece was covered with a protective silver covering to prevent the surface from becoming black due to the smoke from the lamps and candles.

Two other scenes from the life of the Saint recounted in the Painting by Ilario da Viterbo.

The Transitus Chapel

Within the Basilica, at the beginning of the presbytery, on the right, is the very humble, precious hut of the sick friars - the Transitus - that marks the place in which Saint Francis died on the eve of October 3, 1226, at the of 44.

When Saint Francis was sick and living at the residence of the Bishop of Assisi, he felt the end was near and desired to be able to conclude his earthly existence in the place where he had first begun to live the Gospel, so he asked to be taken to the Portiuncula.

Here, stripped of his sackcloth habit and lying naked on the bare ground, Francis dictated his spiritual will and then "welcomed death singing", while a flock of larks chirped loudly. There are frescoes on the outside wall of the Chapel that depict the death and funeral of Saint Francis. They were done in 1886 by the painter Domenico Brushi.

Inside the small room, are paintings of Franciscan saints and blesseds (Saint Juniper, Blessed Philip, Blessed Morico, Blessed Bernard of Assisi, Saint Ottone, Saint Adito, Saint Accursio, Blessed Silvester, Blessed Rufino, Blessed Masseo, Saint Leo, Blessed Giles, Saint Anthony of Padua, Saint Bonaventure, Saint Bernard, Saint Peter the Martyr, Saint Ludovic of Tolosa and Saint Bernardino of Siena). They are the work of the fifteenth century painter, Giovanni di Pietro, known as "Spagna" (1450-1528), one of the closest followers of Perugino.

Inside the Transitus Chapel there is a precious Franciscan relic kept in a reliquary: the cincture of the Saint that girded his waist. It was donated to the Sanctuary by Pope Pius IX (1846-1878).

BONA   VETVRA

S·BERARDVS

The fresco of Giovanni Spagna (ca 1520) depicts the most faithful followers of Francis, those who were his companions from the very beginning.

There is also an important glazed earthenware statue of Saint Francis from around 1475 by Andrea Della Robbia (Florence 1435-1525), nephew of the more famous Luca.

Tradition has it that the mystical meal between Saint Francis and Saint Clare took place in the area around the pillar before the Chapel, during which time a great and marvelous light shown so brightly that the people of Assisi and Bettona rushed en masse to put out the fire that they thought was blazing in that place.

The little cell of the primitive Franciscan infirmary, which was transformed into an oratory immediately after the death of the Saint. On the little altar, is the cord that girdled the waist of the Poverello. It is preserved in an Empire-style reliquary. The glazed earthenware statue of Francis is a work of Andrea della Robbia (1475). In his stigmatized hands, the Saint is holding a crucifix and the Gospels, the two great loves of his whole life.

The "transitus" of Saint Francis. Fresco on the outside wall by D. Bruschi (1886).

Interior
of the Basilica

THE APSE

The large semicircular apse of the Basilica has an impressive wooden choir that was made in the sixteen hundreds by the brothers of Saint Mary of the Angels, under the guidance of Brother Luigi da Selci. The pulpit on the left, which is also made of wood, has valuable baroque carvings that depict episodes of the story of the Pardon. It is the work of Brother Giacomo da Borgo San Sepolcro. The main altar, in Sienese yellow, is decorated with seven bronze panels (Christ among saints Francis, Anthony of Padua, Bonaventure, Clare, Pius V and Pius X). It is a modern work done by Enrico Manfrini, the artist who also did the cross and candlesticks.

The two ambos, located on either side of the steps of the presbytery, are decorated with scenes from the life of Saint Francis. They are the work of the Tyrolese sculptor, Toni Fiedler.

A view of the right nave with the decorated chapels.

THE PAINTINGS OF THE SIDE CHAPELS

There are five chapels along each side of the naves. Starting at the end of the fifteen hundreds, according to an ancient practice, the Franciscans at Saint Mary of the Angels began to assign patrons to the chapels to those who made a request.
Not only were the petitions made by the nobility and middle class, but also by municipal institutions and various religious confraternities

who rushed to make their offer and contribute to decorating the chapels. This was not only a sign of personal devotion to Saint Francis and the Mother of God, but also indicated their social status and preference for a particular art form. Most of the painters who worked in the chapels of Saint Mary of the Angels came from Umbria, but the Basilica became a gathering point of various artistic expressions of different origins.

THE CHAPELS OF THE RIGHT NAVE

Chapel of Saint Anthony the Abbot

The painter Francesco Appiani from The Marches did the frescos that decorate the vault of the Chapel of St. Anthony the Abbot. They depict the cardinal virtues and Saint Anthony the Abbot in glory.

On the right wall of the chapel is the painting of the Baptism of Jesus by Michelangelo da Ponticelli. The fresco on the left wall is of the Miracle of Saint Anthony the Abbot. It was done in 1773 by Antonio Maria Garbi (1718-1797). The altar painting which depicts St. Anthony the Abbot is the work of Giacomo Giorgetti (Assisi 1603-1679), a painter and architect who was

Cappella di Chapel of Saint Anthony the Abbot; vault frescoes by FRANCESCO APPIANI. Above: the altar painting is of *Saint Anthony the Abbot* by GIACOMO GIORGETTI.

Chapel of Saint John the Baptist: vault frescoes by CESARE SERMEI.

Chapel of Saint John the Baptist. *Baptism of Jesus*, altarpiece by CESARE SERMEI.

greatly influenced by Giovanni Lanfranco, one of the greatest painters of the Bolognese school.

Chapel of Saint John the Baptist

In 1608, the task of decorating this chapel was given to the painter Cesare Sermei, who was born in Città della Pieve (Perugia) in 1581 and died in Assisi in 1668.

The frescos on the walls and vault of the chapel depict the Story of the Baptist (left wall: Birth of the Baptist, the Visitation, the Presentation in the Temple, the Annunciation to Zachariah; right wall: the Dance of Salome, the Baptist in prison; the vault: the Trinity, the Preaching and Beheading of the Baptist) and the great altar-piece, the Baptism of Christ.

Sermei painted architecture in prospective to make the best use of space. Twenty years later,

Chapel of Saint John the Baptist: detail of the vault frescoes by CESARE SERMEI.

this painter returned to the Basilica of Saint Mary of the Angels to work in the Chapel of the Stigmata, along with his student Giacomo Giorgetti from Assisi.

Chapel of the Birth of Mary (or Chapel of Saint Ann)

The Chapel of the Birth of Mary (also called the Chapel of Saint Ann) was initially placed under the patronage of the Vigilanti family. It then passed on to the Roncalli family from Bergamo, who paid for the decoration.
It hosts a vast cycle of frescos, done by three painters who worked in the late fifteen hundreds and early sixteen hundreds, all known by the name of "Pomarancio"(from their birth place, the town of Pomarance, near Volterra).

Chapel of the Birth of Mary. ANTONIO CIRCIGNANI, called Pomarancio: *The Wedding Feast of Cana.*

The actual names of the artists are: Niccolò Circignani, Cristoforo Roncalli and Antonio Circignani, son of Niccolò. Because of a rather homogeneous style, their works are easily confused. It seems most probable, however, that the decoration of the Chapel of the Birth of the Virgin was done by Antonio.

On the vault are depicted Pentecost, Jesus among the Doctors, the Wedding Feast of Cana; on the walls are the Presentation of the Virgin

in the Temple, the Annunciation, King David, Salomon, two women prophets and angelic musicians. The young age of the painter, born around 1570, who is depicted in a self-portrait, leads us to believe that the work was done around 1602-1603, the years in which most of the chapels in the Basilica were decorated. The altar-piece with the Birth of the Virgin was executed by Cristoforo Roncalli and is dated between 1606 and 1609.

Chapel of Saint Pius V. BALDASSARRE CROCE, *Descent of the Holy Spirit.*

Chapel of Saint Pius V. BALDASSARRE CROCE, *The Pardon of Assisi.*

Chapel of Pius V

The decoration of this chapel with the Story of the Virgin Mary and the Story of Saint Francis was done by Baldassarre Croce. He was born in Bologna in 1558 where he received his formation and was in contact with the local mannerist environment. In the very early years of the sixteen hundreds, Croce painted the Story of the Virgin Mary (Presentation of Mary in the Temple, Visitation, Assumption) on the vault. A brief cycle of the Story of Saint Francis (Saint Francis in Cannara, the Pardon of Assisi, the Granting of the Pardon, the healing of a child with dropsy) is developed on the walls. In this painting, he tapped into the experience that he had doing his most important works in Rome.

Chapel of the Crib
(previously the Chapel of the Annunciation)

The Chapel of the Annunciation, later called the Chapel of the Crib, was, with all probability, the

Chapel of the Crib.
DOMENICO PACI from
Urbino, *The Crib*.

An interesting view from above the Portiuncula, enclosed within the Basilica of Saint Mary of the Angels.

first to be painted near the end of 1591, when the Basilica was still a work site.

It is difficult to know to whom the works should be attributed. In the past, the frescos on the walls and the vault were attributed to two brothers, Taddeo and Federico Zuccari. The frescoes depict Franciscan stories and they can be dated to the late Perugia Mannerism period, characterized by fading, soft colors.

In place of the altar-piece of the Annunciation, now there is a large crib, the work of Domenico Paci of Urbino.

THE TRANSEPT

The right arm

At the rear of the right arm of the transept is the altar of Saint Peter in Chains, placed under the patronage of the Municipality of Foligno. It is embellished by a monumental group sculpted in plaster, depicting the Freeing of Saint Peter from prison. It is the work of the Belgian sculptor Jean Reinhold, executed in 1675. On the right wall of the transept is the Reliquary Chapel with a wooden cupboard from the XVII century. On the opposite wall is a painting of Christ between Saints Peter of Alcantara and Margaret of Cortona. It was done by Francesco Appiani (1760) who also worked in the Chapel of Saint Anthony the Abbot.

The dome

Three years before painting the right transept, Appiani did the frescos that adorn the great pendentives of the dome and depict Saint Francis renouncing his paternal goods, the Benedictines donating the Portiuncula to Francis, the clothing of Saint Clare, the Meeting of Saint Thomas Aquinas and Saint Bonaventure.

The left arm

The altar of Saint Anthony of Padua is on the back wall of the left transept. It was executed in 1718 and placed under the patronage of the City of Perugia in 1624. The altar bears a large painting depicting the Virgin giving the Child to Saint Anthony of Padua.

The right and left arms of the transept. *Above:* Altar of Saint Peter in Chains. JEAN REINHOLD, *Freeing of Saint Peter from prison. Below:* Altar of Saint Anthony with the painting of the *Virgin giving the Child to Saint Anthony of Padua.*

Chapel of Saint Diego d'Alcalà. ANTONIO MARIA GARBI, *The Glory of Saint Diego*.

THE CHAPELS OF THE LEFT NAVE

Chapel of Saint Diego d'Alcalà

The vault of this Chapel is decorated with frescos depicting the Cardinal virtues and the Glory of Saint Diego. It was done by painter Antonio Maria Garbi, around 1773. The large altar-piece depicting the Miracle of Saint Diego was done around 1710 and is the work of a Franciscan, Ippolito da Coceto. On the right wall is Honorius III granting the Pardon to Francis by Baldassarre Orsini (1787), and on the left wall is Saint Francis announcing the Pardon to the people, by Antonio Cavallucci (1752-1795).

Chapel of the Stigmata

The iconographic plan of this chapel reflects the will of the patron, the Third Order Franciscans, to celebrate Francis as Alter Christus.
Around 1630, the work was entrusted to two local artists, Cesare Sermei (who had already worked in the Chapel of Saint John the Baptist twenty years earlier) and Giacomo Giorgetti, his student.
The frescos on the vault depicting Saint Francis welcomed into Heaven and the Approval of the Rule are the works of Sermei as is the painting on the right wall of the chapel of the Weeping of the Poor Clares. Giorgetti did the large altar-piece depicting the Stigmata of Saint Francis, the painting on the left wall of the scene depicting the Unbelieving Girolamo checking the stigmata of Saint Francis and the fresco on the vault of the episode of Francis giving his tunic to a novice.

Chapel of the Stigmata. CESARE SERMEI, *Saint Francis welcomed into paradise*.

Chapel of the Deposition

The decoration of this chapel (also called the
Chapel of Saint Massimino) was placed under the
patronage of the Breccia-Vigilanti family of Assisi. It
has the work of Baldassarre Croce of Bologna, from
the very first years of the sixteen hundreds, who had
already worked in the Chapel of Pius V, and above
all, of Ventura Salimbeni of Siena (Siena 1568-
1613). In the chapel of the Deposition, Salimbeni

Chapel of the
Deposition.
BALDASSARRE CROCE,
*Deposition from the
cross*.

Chapel of the
Deposition.
VENTURA SALIMBENI,
The Resurrection.

created frescos depicting the Resurrection and the
Pope visiting the dying Saint Clare. Baldassare
Croce (1558-1628) did the large altar-piece,
depicting the Deposition from the Cross, the fresco
on the vault of the Clothing of Saint Clare, of which
the preparatory designs were the work of Salimbeni.
Two other paintings in the chapel, the Risen
Christ presenting those freed from Limbo to the
Virgin and Christ's farewell to the Blessed Mother,
are attributed to Piergirolamo Crispolti, who
worked in the first half of the sixteen hundreds.

Chapel of the Coronation of the B.V. Mary

The decoration of the entire chapel was done
by Simeone Ciburri, a painter from Perugia who
worked between the end of the fifteen hundreds and
the first quarter of the sixteen hundreds. The signed
altar-piece named the Assumption and Coronation
of the Blessed Virgin Mary can be dated to 1603.

On the right wall is the painting of Saint Diego healing the son of the King of Spain, also signed and dated 1603. The decoration of this chapel was the most prestigious commission obtained by Ciburri. He also produced six other paintings placed on two pillars at the entrance, with Angels, Virtues and Saints, and six others on the vault that depict the Eternal and the Glory of Angels and Saints.

Chapel of the Coronation of the Blessed Virgin Mary. SIMEONE CIBURRI, *The Eternal and the glory of angels and saints*.

Chapel of Our Lady of the Rosary (or Chapel of Saint Rufino)

The interior of this chapel is dominated by an imposing altar picture of Our Lady of the Rosary with Saints Rufino and Anthony the Abbot, done by Domenico Maria Muratori, a painter who worked in the eighteenth century.
On the right wall there is a painting depicting Galeazzo Alessi presenting the plans for the Basilica to Pius V. It was done by Baldassarre Orsini who had also worked in the Chapel of Saint Diego d'Alcalà. A repainted fresco, by the Umbrian painter Carlo Ventura Morelli, depicts The Glory of Saint Rufino.

The Rose Garden

This area of the Sanctuary is what remains of the ancient woods where the brothers lived. This is the place where Saint Francis lived his daily life as a man who encountered God and lived in his love.

Francis spoke as a friend to a cricket, with whom he took turns singing praise to the Lord for an entire week. When he passed by the sheep ran happily and joyously to greet him, and at the Portiuncula, there was a little sheep that followed him everywhere and bleated in union with the brothers praying in the little church.

He told the birds to thank the providential God who cares for them with their flight and song and invited them to praise Him. They gave signs of happy approval.

CHAPEL OF THE ROSES

This is the place of the original hut where Francis lived. It had already been made into a chapel in 1260 and was enlarged to make the current Chapel of the Roses in about 1440. It was also called the "Hermitage of Saint Francis" or the Chapel of the Roses. The place is named for the patch of little roses without thorns that grows nearby. The Saint threw himself into a hedge of thorns to get rid of doubts and temptations and the hedge miraculously changed into thornless roses, giving origin to Rosa canina Assisiensis which continue to flower today. The interior of the small oratory is decorated with frescos by Tiberio d'Assisi, who died in 1524.

Oratory of the roses, including the place where Francis lived, under the altar.

Rose garden: with the statue of Saint Francis and the doves that nest in his hands.

The first cycle of frescos on the upper level shows Saint Francis and his twelve companions, together with Saint Clare and Saint Elisabeth of Hungary, with Saints Bonaventure of Bagnoregio, Bernardino of Siena, Ludovic of Tolosa and Anthony of Padua. On the vault is the image of the Eternal giving His blessing, surrounded by cherubim. It was executed by Tiberio d'Assisi in 1506, as attested by the inscription "MDVI die prima augusti". In the lower area is a brief cycle, also done by Tiberio d'Assisi in 1518, of the Story of the Pardon obtained at the Portiuncula: Apparition of the angels to Saint Francis lying among the thorns of the rose garden, Saint Francis guided by the angels to the Portiuncula, Apparition of Christ to the Virgin, Pope Honorius III giving the Indulgence, Proclamation of the indulgence by Saint Francis.

An aspect of great interest in the fresco of the Proclamation of the Indulgence by Saint Francis is that the work portrays the buildings that existed around the Portiuncula at the beginning of the fifteen hundreds, before the construction of the huge Basilica.

Under the Chapel is a sort of grotto with a small statue of Saint Francis in prayer and the remnants of the beams which, according to tradition, were used to make the improvised pulpit from which the Saint, in the presence of seven Umbrian bishops, announced the great privilege of the Indulgence to the crowd of pilgrims. According to tradition, it is also said that the meeting between Francis and Saint Anthony of Padua took place here.

V. Rosugnoli (1916). The bronze statue depicts an episode when a lamb was given to Saint Francis.

The walls of the Chapel of the Roses with the frescoes of Tiberio di Assisi (1506-1516).

The Portiuncula Museum

The museum of the Basilica of Saint Mary of the Angels, located next to the Sanctuary, was opened in June of 2000.

In the first room (A), there is a model of the landscape of the Portiuncula as it appeared during the time of Saint Francis. An Etruscan urn, a Roman stele and above all an interesting stone plaque from the IX-X century, the oldest remains of the place, are also in this room. The next room (B) is dominated by the precious cross of Giunta Pisano, depicting Christus patiens, where Christ hangs lifeless from the wood of the cross.

The Franciscans were among the main diffusers of this particular iconograph done in eastern Byzantine style between the IX and XI centuries, because it emphasized the human nature of Christ sacrificed for the redemption of man.

The icon of the Master of Saint Francis, the oldest image of the saint preserved at the Portiuncula, is also in this room. It is probable that the painting was displayed in the place where he died on the evening of October 3, 1226, to remind the pilgrims of the stigmatized saint and to propose it as a relic for the devotion of the faithful. According to tradition, the body of Francis was laid on top of it when he was taken from the Portiuncula to Assisi for burial.

In the room there is a striking image of Saint Francis attributed to Cimabue.

The fourteen hundreds room (C) documents

how the spiritual value of the Portiuncula became
even more intense after the death of Francis. The
little church is the most authentic witness of the
life and message of the saint.
At the beginning of the fourteen hundreds the
fundamental principle of primitive Franciscanism
was relaunched by the Observants, of whom the
major proponent was Saint Bernardino of Siena
(1380-1444). The wooden pulpit said to be that
of Saint Bernardino and the monograms of the

Our Lady of the Milk.
(XIV century).

Preceding page:
GIUNTA PISANO,
Crucifix, 1236..

Page 54:
ANDREA DELLA
ROBBIA, *Coronation
of the Blessed Virgin
Mary*, 1475..

MASTER OF SAINT
FRANCIS, *Saint Francis*
(detail), XIII Century.

Name of Jesus (HIS), a devotion practiced and
spread by the saint, belong to this period.
The valuable ornamental altar piece of the
Coronation of the Blessed Virgin Mary by Andrea
della Robbia was done around 1475 and is indicative
of the growing desire to embellish the complex of the
Portiuncula with prestigious furnishings (room C).
After passing through what remains of the ancient
fifteenth century cloister, one enters the ancient
refectory, now dedicated to Marian iconography
(D). Francis had a unique understanding of the
role that Mary played in salvation history. In fact,
he understood the Portiuncula to be not only a
"little portion" of the world entrusted to him by
God to serve him, but he also saw it as the figure
of the Virgin, the holy and elect "little portion" of

FEDERICO BAROCCI,
Annunciation, 1596..

humanity, chosen by the Father for the Incarnate Word. Numerous works of the image of Mary at the Portiuncula are in room D, the most notable being "Our Lady of the Milk". The sculpture from the end of the fourteenth century was originally placed in the gothic-style niche above the façade of the Portiuncula. It was partially destroyed in the 1832 earthquake. Recent restoration revealed traces of the original colors: red and black for the clothing of the Virgin and Child and green at the base of the throne. One can see what the decorations of the altar of the Portiuncula looked like at the beginning of the nineteen hundreds based on designs done by Francesco Providoni in 1687 and on a series of copper engravings from the eighteen hundreds.

Silver,
Reliquary cross,
XIV century.

SANO DI PIETRO,
The Blessed Mother with Child,
XV century.

CIMABUE, *Saint Francis.*
The work is proof that
this artist was working
for the brothers of the
Portiuncula very close
to the time that the
transept of the Basilica
of Saint Francis of Assisi
was being frescoed..

Until the eighteen hundreds the Marian image was entirely concealed and was only shown to the faithful on major feasts of the year. On these rare occasions, the Virgin was uncovered for the faithful to venerate, by opening the silver covering that protected her. The ones currently in exposition were done in 1802, after the originals were taken by Napoleon's troops in 1798.

Room E is dedicated to the Alessian Basilica (1569-1679), in which interesting documents from the Portiuncula archives have been displayed for the first time. There are designs of the dome and its wooden model as well as preparatory plaster studies of the altars in the transepts. There is a large painting of Saint John of Capestrano and Saint Pasqual Baylon, which was done in 1692 by Francesco Providoni on the occasion of their canonization. Two paintings of Saint Francis and Saint Clare are the works of Cesare Sermei. He was born in Città della Pieve in 1581 and moved to Assisi in 1607, where he did most of his work. A small part of the Museum shows the events associated with the 1832 earthquake that caused the partial collapse of the Basilica and its reconsecration by Cardinal Lambruschini on September 8, 1840.

The exposition is located on the first floor in the corridor that leads into the little convent. It is possible to see a plaster model of the current monumental façade, projected by Bazzani in 1925, as well as plaster models of the statues that decorate it.

The recently repaired (2000) small convent gives an idea of the architecture that was typical of the Observant convents and even though it is not completely original, because it was partially rebuilt, it is extremely interesting.

Index

Printed by Grafiche VD srl
Città di Castello (PG), Italy
grafichevd@gmail.com